THE CHRISTMAS STORY

This book belongs to

_____

Merry Christmas!

Love,

Mrs. Cook &
Mrs. Martino

The Christmas Story

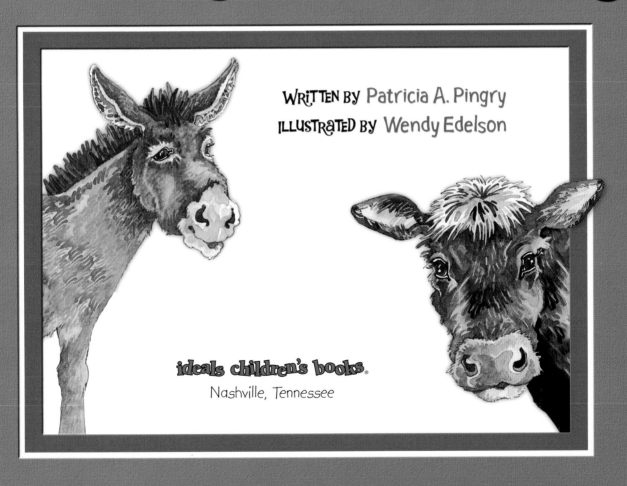

WRITTEN BY Patricia A. Pingry

ILLUSTRATED BY Wendy Edelson

ideals children's books®

Nashville, Tennessee

ISBN-13: 978-0-8249-5512-0
ISBN-10: 0-8249-5512-9

Published by Ideals Children's Books
An imprint of Ideals Publications
A Guideposts Company
Nashville, Tennessee
www.idealsbooks.com

Color separations by Precision Color Graphics, Franklin, Wisconsin
Printed and bound in China

Library of Congress Cataloging-in-Publication Data

Pingry, Patricia A., date.
  The Christmas story / written by Patricia A. Pingry ; illustrated by
Wendy Edelson.
    p. cm.
  "An Ideals Christmas classic."
  Originally published: Nashville, Tenn. : CandyCane Press, c2004
  ISBN-13: 978-0-8249-5512-0
  ISBN-10: 0-8249-5512-9 (pbk. : alk. paper)
  1. Jesus Christ—Nativity—Juvenile literature. I. Edelson, Wendy. II.
Title.
  BT315.P54 2005
  232.92—dc22
                              2005009110

Designed by Georgina Chidlow-Rucker

For Abigail

Leo_Jul11_9

On
Christmas,
we celebrate
the birth of
Jesus Christ
our Savior.
This is the
Christmas story.

Many years ago, a man named Joseph and his wife, Mary, lived in Nazareth. One day, they had to take a trip.

Mary rode on a
donkey.
Joseph
walked
by her side.

They came to
a town called
Bethlehem.
They looked for
a place to
sleep.
There were
so many people,
there was no
room
for Mary
and Joseph.

Finally, an
innkeeper
said they could
stay in his
stable.
Joseph made a
soft
bed for Mary.
They lay down
to sleep.

During the night, Mary's **baby** was born. She **wrapped** him in soft cloths and laid him in the **manger.** She called him "**Jesus.**"

In a
field
not far away,
shepherds
were watching
their sheep.
Suddenly, an
angel
appeared. The
shepherds were
afraid.

The angel said, "Do not be afraid. I have **good** news! A Savior has been born in Bethlehem. You will find **him** lying in a **manger.**"

Then there were many angels. They said, "Glory to God in the highest, and on earth peace, goodwill toward men."

After
the angels left,
the shepherds ran to
Bethlehem.
They were
looking
for the
Savior.

When the
shepherds
found
the manger,
they
worshiped
the
baby,
Jesus.

This is the **Christmas** story. Jesus **Christ** our Savior was **born** in Bethlehem and found **lying** in a manger.

The Real Christmas Story

Luke 2:1-16

And it came to pass in those days, that there went out a decree from Caesar Augustus that all the world should be taxed.... And all went to be taxed, every one into his own city.

And Joseph also went up from Galilee, out of the city of Nazareth, into Judaea, unto the city of David, which is called Bethlehem; (because he was of the house and lineage of David:) To be taxed with Mary his espoused wife, being great with child.

And so it was, that, while they were there, the days were accomplished that she should be delivered. And she brought forth her firstborn son, and wrapped him in swaddling clothes, and laid him in a manger; because there was no room for them in the inn.

And there were in the same country shepherds abiding in the field, keeping watch over their flock by night. And, lo, the angel of the Lord came upon them, and the glory of the Lord shone round about them: and they were sore afraid.

And the angel said unto them, Fear not: for, behold, I bring you good tidings of great joy, which shall be to all people. For unto you is born this day in the city of David a Saviour, which is Christ the Lord. And this shall be a sign unto you; Ye shall find the babe wrapped in swaddling clothes, lying in a manger.

And suddenly there was with the angel a multitude of the heavenly host praising God, and saying, Glory to God in the highest, and on earth peace, good will toward men.

And it came to pass, as the angels were gone away from them into heaven, the shepherds said one to another, Let us now go even unto Bethlehem, and see this thing which is come to pass, which the Lord hath made known unto us. And they came with haste, and found Mary, and Joseph, and the babe lying in a manger.